VALENTINE'S DAY JOKES for Kids

270 Clean, Silly, and Hilarious Jokes

By

GUS GLIMMER

Thank you for selecting our Valentine's Day Jokes for Kids for your little one! We sincerely hope our book brings joy and laughter to your family.

We would greatly appreciate it if you could take a moment to share your thoughts by leaving a review. Your feedback is incredibly valuable to us, aiding in our continuous improvement and enabling us to reach more families seeking delightful resources.

Once again, thank you for choosing our Valentine's Day Jokes for Kids. We eagerly anticipate hearing your thoughts and those of your kids!

THIS BOOK
BELONGS TO

_ _ _ _ _ _ _ _ _ _ _ _ _ _ _ _ _

_ _ _ _ _ _ _ _ _ _ _ _ _ _ _ _ _

WHAT DID ONE PENCIL SAY TO THE OTHER ON VALENTINE'S DAY?

You're write for me!

WHY DID THE BICYCLE FALL IN LOVE?

Because it was two-tired of being alone!

HOW DID THE PHONE PROPOSE TO HIS GIRLFRIEND?

He gave her a ring

WHAT DID THE EARTH SAY TO THE SUN?

You light up my world!

WHAT DID THE ALIEN SAY TO HIS SWEETHEART ON VALENTINE'S DAY?

You're out of this world!

WHAT DID THE LIGHTBULB SAY TO HIS GIRLFRIEND?

I love you a whole watt!

KNOCK, KNOCK

Who's there?

Honeydew.

Honeydew who?

Honeydew you know how much I love you?

WHAT DID ONE VOLCANO SAY TO THE OTHER?

I lava you a lot!

WHAT DID THE PENCIL SAY TO THE ERASER ON VALENTINE'S DAY?

You make all my mistakes disappear!

WHY DID THE SCARECROW BECOME A GREAT VALENTINE'S DAY POET?

Because he was outstanding in his field!

WHAT DID ONE SNOWMAN SAY TO THE SUN ON VALENTINE'S DAY?

You melt my heart!

HOW DID THE COMPUTER EXPRESS LOVE?

It sent a heartfelt byte!

HOW DO YOU KNOW WHEN A JOKE IS IN LOVE?

It's corny!

WHAT DID THE ZERO SAY TO THE EIGHT ON VALENTINE'S DAY?

Nice belt!

WHAT DID THE STAMP SAY TO THE ENVELOPE ON VALENTINE'S DAY?

I'm stuck on you!

HOW DID THE TELESCOPE ASK OUT THE MICROSCOPE ON VALENTINE'S DAY?

I've got my eyes on you!

KNOCK, KNOCK

Who's there?

Lettuce.

Lettuce who?

Lettuce be together on Valentine's Day!

WHAT DID DOOR SAY TO THE KEY ON VALENTINE'S DAY?

You unlock my heart!

KNOCK, KNOCK

Who's there?

Icy.

Icy who?

Icy you're the one for me this Valentine's Day!

WHAT DID ONE OCEAN SAY TO THE OTHER OCEAN ON VALENTINE'S DAY?

Nothing, they just waved!

WHY DID THE ALIEN BREAK UP WITH HIS GIRLFRIEND?

They needed space!

WHAT DID ONE SHOE SAY TO THE OTHER ON VALENTINE'S DAY?

You're the perfect fit for my sole!

KNOCK, KNOCK

Who's there?

Luke

Luke who?

Luke who got a Valentine!

WHAT DID THE ONE SHEEP SAY TO THE OTHER?

I love ewe!

WHAT DO OWLS SAY TO DECLARE THEIR LOVE?

Owl be yours!

WHAT DID THE BOY SQUIRREL SAY TO THE GIRL SQUIRREL ON VALENTINE'S DAY?

I'm nuts about you!

WHAT DID ONE WATERMELON SAY TO THE OTHER ON VALENTINE'S DAY?

You're one in a melon!

WHAT DID ONE PLATE SAY TO THE OTHER ON VALENTINE'S DAY?

We make the perfect pair!

WHY DID THE BALLOON BREAK UP WITH THE HELIUM TANK?

It needed space!

HOW DID THE TELEPHONE PROPOSE TO THE SMARTPHONE?

I've got to call you mine!

WHAT DID ONE OCEAN SAY TO THE OTHER?

You're shorely the one for me!

WHAT DID THE PAPER CLIP SAY TO THE DOCUMENT ON VALENTINE'S DAY?

Let's stay attached forever!

WHAT DID THE CANDY SAY TO ITS WRAPPER ON VALENTINE'S DAY?

You make me look sweet!

WHAT DID THE SALT SAY TO THE PEPPER ON VALENTINE'S DAY?

You spice up my life!

WHY DID THE BANANA GO TO THE VALENTINE'S DAY PARTY?

Because it had appeal!

WHAT DO YOU CALL TWO BIRDS IN LOVE?

Tweethearts!

HOW DID THE SALAD EXPRESS ITS LOVE ON VALENTINE'S DAY?

It said, "Lettuce romaine together forever!"

WHAT DID THE SPAGHETTI SAY TO THE MEATBALL ON VALENTINE'S DAY?

You're saucy and I'm falling for you!

WHAT DID THE BEE SAY TO THE FLOWER ON VALENTINE'S DAY?

Bee mine!

WHAT DO YOU SAY TO AN OCTOPUS ON VALENTINE'S DAY?

I want to hold your hand, hand, hand, hand, hand, hand, hand, hand!

WHY DO SKUNKS LOVE VALENTINE'S DAY?

They are very scent-imental creatures

WHY DID THE SHERIFF LOCK UP HER BOYFRIEND?

He stole her heart

WHAT DID ONE JEDI SAY TO THE OTHER ON VALENTINE'S DAY?

Yoda one for me!

WHAT DID THE REFRIGERATOR SAY TO THE MAGNET?

I find you very attractive

WHAT DID ONE BLUEBERRY SAY TO THE OTHER ON VALENTINE'S DAY?

I love you berry much

WHAT DID ONE CRAYON SAY TO THE OTHER ON VALENTINE'S DAY?

You color my world with love!

WHAT DID THE TOOTHBRUSH SAY TO THE TOOTHPASTE ON VALENTINE'S DAY?

You make my smile sparkle!

HOW DID THE BOOK EXPRESS ITS LOVE ON VALENTINE'S DAY?

It opened up and revealed its heartfelt words!

WHY DID THE BROOM TAKE THE VACUUM CLEANER TO DINNER ON VALENTINE'S DAY?

It wanted a sweep date!

WHY DID THE CRAB NEVER SHARE ITS VALENTINE'S DAY CARDS?

Because it was a little shellfish!

WHY DID THE CAT SIT ON THE COMPUTER ON VALENTINE'S DAY?

It wanted to keep an eye on the mouse!

Who's there?

Will.

Will who?

Will you be my Valentine?

Who's there?

Russian.

Russian who?

I'm Russian to get your phone number.

Who's there?

Water

Water who?

Water you doing later tonight?

Who's there?

Howard

Howard who?

Howard you like to be my Valentine?

Who's there?

Wendy

Wendy who?

Wendy you think we can go on a date?

Who's there?

Peas.

Peas who?

Peas be my Valentine.

WHAT DID ONE SNOWFLAKE SAY TO THE OTHER ON VALENTINE'S DAY?

You're one-of-a-kind

HOW DID THE CALCULATOR PROPOSE TO THE RULER ON VALENTINE'S DAY?

Let's measure our love!

HOW DID THE LITTLE RAINDROP PROPOSE TO THE PUDDLE.

Let's stick together

WHY DID THE COFFEE FILE A POLICE REPORT ON VALENTINE'S DAY?

It got mugged!

WHAT DID THE PAINTER TELL HIS GIRLFRIEND?

I love you with all my art

WHAT DID THE SCIENTIST SAY TO HER VALENTINE?

I think of you periodically

LOVE

WHAT DID ONE CAT SAY TO THE OTHER CAT ON VALENTINE'S DAY?

You're purr-fect

DO YOU HAVE A DATE FOR VALENTINE'S DAY?

Yes, it's February 14.

WHO ALWAYS HAS A DATE ON VALENTINE'S DAY?

A calendar

WHAT DID ONE MIRROR SAY TO THE OTHER ON VALENTINE'S DAY?

You reflect the best in me

HOW DID THE ICEBERG PROPOSE TO THE GLACIER ON VALENTINE'S DAY?

Let's melt each other's hearts!

WHAT DID ONE OAR TELL THE OTHER OAR?

This is so row-mantic!

WHAT DID THE COUPLE SAY AFTER THEY WERE STRUCK BY CUPID'S ARROW?

"Ouch!"

WHY DID THE SKELETON BREAK UP WITH HER BOYFRIEND ON VALENTINE'S DAY?

Her heart wasn't in it.

WHAT DO YOU CALL A COLORFUL HEART THAT LOVES BOOKS?

Well-red

HOW DO RAINBOWS EXPRESS THEIR LOVE ON VALENTINE'S DAY?

they paint the sky with hues of happiness!

WHAT DID THE WOMAN WITH A BROKEN LEG TELL HER VALENTINE?

I have a crutch on you.

WHAT DID THE CALCULATOR SAY TO THE PENCIL ON VALENTINE'S DAY?

You can count on me.

WHAT DID THE BEE SAY TO ITS VALENTINE AFTER A DATE?

You're the beest company!

HOW DID THE MOON CONFESS ITS FEELINGS TO THE SUN?

It said, "You light up my night!"

WHAT DO FARMERS GIVE FOR VALENTINE'S DAY?

Lots of hogs and kisses.

WHAT DID THE WHALE SAY TO HIS SWEETHEART ON VALENTINE'S DAY?

Whale you be mine?

Who's there?

Al.

Al who?

Al be your Valentine if you'll be mine

WHAT DID ONE SCIENTIST SAY TO THE OTHER?

We've got good chemistry.

KNOCK, KNOCK

Who's there?

Orange.

Orange who?

Orange you glad to be my Valentine?

HOW DID THE LETTUCE ASK THE SPINACH OUT ON A DATE?

Here's my number so kale me maybe?

WHAT'S THE MOST ROMANTIC SEA CREATURE?

A cuddlefish.

WHEN DO BED BUGS FALL IN LOVE?

In the spring.

WHAT DID ONE PIECE OF TOAST SAY TO THE OTHER?

"You're my butter half!"

WHY IS LETTUCE THE MOST LOVING VEGETABLE?

Because it's all heart

WHAT DID ONE FLAME SAY TO THE OTHER ON VALENTINE'S DAY?

We're a perfect match!

WHY DID THE CELL PHONE GET A VALENTINE'S DAY CARD?

Because it had a great connection!

WHAT DID THE COMPUTER SAY TO ITS VALENTINE?

"You've got a byte of my heart!

WHY DID THE PENCIL DRAW HEARTS ALL OVER THE PAPER?

It was sketching its love!

HOW DID THE FLOWER PROPOSE TO THE GRASS ON VALENTINE'S DAY?

Let's grow together

WHY DID THE TEDDY BEAR PROPOSE TO THE PLUSH BUNNY?

it can't bear to be without it!

WHAT DID THE CUCUMBER SAY TO HIS FRIEND?

You mean a great dill to me.

WHY DID THE PUZZLE PIECES GO ON A DATE ON VALENTINE'S DAY?

They fit together perfectly!

WHAT DID ONE CAMERA SAY TO THE OTHER ON VALENTINE'S DAY?

"You always capture my heart!"

WHAT DID THE CRAYON SAY TO THE COLORING BOOK ON VALENTINE'S DAY?

"Together, we make a masterpiece!"

WHAT DID ONE FEATHER SAY TO THE OTHER ON VALENTINE'S DAY?

"You tickle my fancy"

WHAT DID THE CELL PHONE SAY TO ITS CHARGER?

"You complete my charge!"

WHAT DID ONE PILLOW SAY TO THE OTHER?

"You're my soft spot"

WHAT DID THE CLOCK SAY TO THE CALENDAR ON VALENTINE'S DAY?

"I'm ready to spend all my time with you!"

WHAT DID THE GHOST SAY TO HIS WIFE ON VALENTINE'S DAY?

"You look so BOOtiful."

WHAT DID THE RABBIT SAY TO HIS GIRLFRIEND ON VALENTINE'S DAY?

"Somebunny loves you"

WHAT DID THE BAKER SAY TO HIS SWEETHEART?

I'm dough-nuts about you!

WHAT DID THE DRUM SAY TO THE OTHER ON VALENTINE'S DAY?

"My heart beats for you"

HOW DID THE TRAIN SAY TO THE OTHER ON VALENTINE'S DAY?

"I choo-choo-choose you!"

HOW DID THE CLOUD PROPOSE TO THE RAINDROP?

It said,"Let's shower the world with our love!"

WHAT DID THE FIREFLY SAY TO ITS VALENTINE?

"You light up my night!"

WHY DID THE BOOK BREAK UP WITH THE BOOKMARK?

It felt they were on different pages!

WHAT DID THE EARTH SAY TO THE MOON ON VALENTINE'S DAY?

"Our love is written in the stars!"

HOW DID THE COMPUTER MOUSE EXPRESS LOVE TO THE KEYBOARD?

It said, "You click with me"

WHAT DID THE RADIO SAY TO ITS VALENTINE?

Our love is always in tune!

HOW DID THE CLOUD ASK THE SUN TO BE ITS VALENTINE?

It said, "Shine your love on me!"

HOW DO SNAKES EXPRESS AFFECTION?

With love and hisses

WHY DID EVERYONE WANT TO BE BANANA'S VALENTINE?

She is very a-peeling.

WHAT DID ONE PIE SAY TO THE OTHER ON VALENTINE'S DAY?

Pie like you berry much

WHAT DID THE NEEDLE SAY TO THE THREAD?

You're sew special to me

HOW DO SHEEP REPLY AFTER HEARING "I LOVE YOU"?

You're not so baaa-d yourself.

WHY SHOULD YOU DATE A GOALIE?

They're a real keeper.

WHAT FLOWER GIVES THE MOST KISSES ON VALENTINE'S DAY?

Tulips (tow-lips)

WHAT DID ONE TREE SAY TO THE OTHER ON VALENTINE'S DAY?

Do you be-leaf in love?

KNOCK, KNOCK

Who's there?
Oil.
Oil who?
Oil love you forever.

WHAT DID THE MAILBOX SAY TO THE LETTER ON VALENTINE'S DAY?

"You've got mail — and my heart!"

WHAT DID THE NOSE SAY TO THE ROSE ON VALENTINE'S DAY?

You smell lovely

WHAT DID THE GPS SAY TO THE MAP ON VALENTINE'S DAY?

I'm lost without you

WHAT DID ONE OCEAN SAY TO TO ITS VALENTINE?

Our love runs deep

WHAT DID THE 0 SAY TO THE 1?

Without you I'm nothing.

WHAT DID THE MATH BOOK SAY TO THE NOTEBOOK ON VALENTINE'S DAY?

Together, we make the perfect equation!

WHAT DID THE EGG SAY TO THE FRYING PAN ON VALENTINE'S DAY?

You really know how to crack me up

KNOCK, KNOCK

Who's there?

Kenya

Kenya who?

Kenya be my Valentine already.

KNOCK, KNOCK

Who's there?

Beak

Beak who?

Beak careful with my heart.

KNOCK, KNOCK

Who's there?

Fur

Fur who?

Fur you, I'd do anything.

KNOCK, KNOCK

Who's there?

Mustache

Mustache who?

I mustache you to be mine.

KNOCK, KNOCK

Who's there?

Love.

Love who?

Aw, love you too.

KNOCK, KNOCK

Who's there?

Butter.

Butter who?

Butter together than apart.

Who's there?

Anita.

Anita who?

Anita tell you that I love you.

Who's there?

Cows go.

Cows go who?

No silly, cows go "moo," but on Valentine's Day, I go "I love you

Who's there?

Teddy.

Teddy who?

Teddy is Valentine's Day.

KNOCK, KNOCK

Who's there?

Atch.

Atch who?

Bless you! I must be catching feelings for you

KNOCK, KNOCK

Who's there?

Alpaca.

Alpaca who?

Alpaca the chocolates; you take the flowers on Valentine's Day!

KNOCK, KNOCK

Who's there?

Donut.

Donut who?

Donut forget to be my Valentine!

WHAT DID ONE PLATE SAY TO THE OTHER ON VALENTINE'S DAY?

Lunch is on me!

HOW DO YOU ORGANIZE A FANTASTIC SPACE VALENTINE'S DAY PARTY?

You planet!

WHY DID THE TEDDY BEAR SAY NO TO DESSERT ON VALENTINE'S DAY?

It was already stuffed!

WHY DID THE BEE HAVE A VALENTINE'S DAY WEDDING?

Because it found its honey!

HOW DID THE SNOWMAN ASK THE SNOWWOMAN OUT ON VALENTINE'S DAY?

It said, "I've fallen for you, snow and steady!"

WHAT DID THE GRAPE SAY TO THE RAISIN ON VALENTINE'S DAY?

You raisin my heart rate!

WHAT DO BUNNIES DO AFTER THEY GET MARRIED?

Go on a bunnymoon!

WHAT DID THE TORTOISE SAY ON VALENTINE'S DAY?

I turt-ally love you

HOW CAN YOU GET ARRESTED ON VALENTINE'S DAY?

For stealing someone's heart

IF HE DOESN'T APPRECIATE YOUR FRUIT JOKES, YOU NEED TO LET THAT MANGO

KNOCK, KNOCK

Who's there?

Disguise

Disguise who?

Disguise is your boy friend!

WHAT DID THE BOY BAT SAY TO THE GIRL BAT ON VALENTINE'S DAY?

You're fun to hang around with!

WHY DID THE ROOSTER GET A TATTOO?

He wanted to impress the chicks!

WHAT DID ONE PIECE OF STRING SAY TO THE OTHER ON VALENTINE'S DAY?

I'm totally knotty about you!

WHAT DID THE BLANKET SAY TO THE BED ON VALENTINE'S DAY?

You're my cuddle partner

WHAT DID ONE BALLOON SAY TO THE OTHER ON VALENTINE'S DAY?

Love is in the air!

HOW DO YOU MAKE A TISSUE DANCE ON VALENTINE'S DAY?

You put a little boogie in it!

WHY DID THE COOKIE GO TO THE DOCTOR ON VALENTINE'S DAY?

It was feeling a little crumbly!

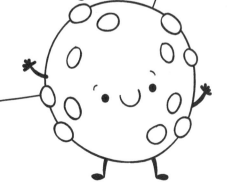

WHAT DID ONE FLOWER SAY TO THE OTHER ON VALENTINE'S DAY?

I'm blooming for you!

WHAT DID ONE BOOK SAY TO THE OTHER ON VALENTINE'S DAY?

You're a novel companion!

WHY DID THE TOMATO TURN RED ON VALENTINE'S DAY?

Because it saw the salad dressing!

HOW DO YOU MAKE A VALENTINE'S DAY EGG LAUGH?

Tell it a yolk!

HOW DID THE COIN PROPOSE TO HIS GIRLFRIEND?

He gave her a jingle

WHAT DO YOU CALL TWO SPARROWS WHO JUST GOT ENGAGED?

Lovebirds

HOW DID THE TWO PRUNES CONFIRM DINNER PLANS?

They said it was a date.

WHAT DID ONE CAPPUCCINO SAY TO THEIR SHY CRUSH?

Espresso yourself

HOW DID THE VEGETABLE POLITELY ASK FOR A DATE?

Peas be my Valentine

WHAT DID THE BAKER SAY TO HIS WIFE ON V-DAY?

Gimme some sugar!

WHAT DO YOU CALL SOMEONE WITH A COLD ON VALENTINE'S DAY?

Lovesick

HOW DOES CUPID DELIVER VALENTINE'S ALL OVER THE WORLD?

On an arrow-plane

XOXO

WHAT TWO WORDS HAVE A THOUSAND LETTERS IN THEM ON VALENTINE'S DAY?

Post Office

WHAT DID THE BEET SAY TO THEIR VALENTINE?

You make my heart beet faster!

WHAT WOULD A MUSHROOM TELL THEIR VALENTINE?

I have so mushroom in my heart for you

WHY WAS THE GHOST SAD ON VALENTINE'S DAY?

He didn't have a boo.

WHAT DID ONE PIG SAY TO THE OTHER?

Don't go bacon my heart.

DID YOU HEAR ABOUT THE TWO RADIOS THAT GOT MARRIED?

The reception was amazing

WHAT'S A BREAD LOAF'S FAVORITE SONG?

"All You Knead is Love."

WHAT DO YOU CALL TWO SPIDERS WHO JUST GOT MARRIED?

Newly-webs

WHAT DO YOU CALL IT WHEN TWO BOATS FALL IN LOVE?

A row-mance.

WHY SHOULDN'T YOU FALL IN LOVE WITH A PASTRY CHEF?

They'll dessert you.

WHAT DID ONE TOMATO SAY TO THE OTHER ON VALENTINE'S DAY?

I love you from my head to-ma-toes.

WHAT DID ONE TOAD SAY TO THE OTHER?

Never frog-et how much I love you

WHAT DID THE DOORBELL GIVE TO HIS GIRLFRIEND?

A ring

WHY DID THE BICYCLE INVITE THE TRICYCLE TO THE VALENTINE'S DAY PARTY?

It wanted a wheely good time!

WHAT SHOULD YOU WRITE ON A SLUG'S VALENTINE CARD?

Happy Valen-SLIME!

HOW DID THE APPLE EXPRESS LOVE TO THE ORANGE?

It said, "We may be apples and oranges, but we're still fruitfully in love!"

WHAT DID THE SNOWFLAKE SAY TO THE ICICLE ON VALENTINE'S DAY?

Together, we make winter wonderful!

HOW DID THE MOON EXPRESS LOVE TO THE EARTH?

It said, "You're my world"

WHY DID THE VALENTINE'S DAY CARD GET IN TROUBLE AT SCHOOL?

It couldn't stop passing notes!

WHAT DID ONE TREE SAY TO THE OTHER ON VALENTINE'S DAY?

Our love is evergreen!

WHAT DID THE LATTE SAY TO THE ESPRESSO?

We are meant to bean

WHY DID THE ASTRONAUT COUPLE BREAK UP?

They needed space

WHAT DID ONE SHEEP SAY TO THE OTHER?

Ewe complete me

WHAT DID A COOK SAY TO ANOTHER ON VALENTINE'S DAY?

You bake me crazy

KNOCK, KNOCK

Who's there?

Justin.

Justin who?

Justin case you didn't know,
you're my Valentine!

WHAT DID THE TRIANGLE SAY TO HIS GIRLFRIEND ON VALENTINE'S DAY?

You look acute

HOW DID THE BROOM GET A GIRLFRIEND?

He swept her off her feet!

WHERE DID THE HAMBURGER TAKE HIS DATE FOR VALENTINE'S DAY?

The meatball

WHAT DO MONKEYS SAY TO THEIR LOVED ONES?

I'm bananas for you!

HOW DOES A BEEKEEPER ASK FOR A VALENTINE?

Would you bee my honey?

WHY DOES MEXICAN FOOD ALWAYS HAVE THE BEST TIME ON A DATE?

It always has something to taco bout!

WHY ARE SUSHI AND CHOPSTICKS THE PERFECT MATCH?

They are soy-mates!

WHY DO SOCCER PLAYERS DISLIKE VALENTINE'S DAY?

They hate getting red cards.

WHAT DID THE TYRANNOSAURUS REX SAY TO HIS LADY LOVE?

You are dino-mite!

HOW DO LIONS EXPRESS THEIR LOVE?

They talk about their felines!

HOW DOES A COKE ASK OUT A SPRITE?

He tells her she is soda-rn cute!

HOW DID THE SNOWFLAKE EXPRESS LOVE TO THE ICICLE?

"You're the coolest Valentine ever!"

WHAT'S CUPID'S FAVORITE SUPERHERO TV SHOW?

Arrow

WHAT'S THE MOST ROMANTIC PART OF A FORK?

Its Valen-tines

HOW DOES A THUNDERSTORM COMPLIMENT LIGHTNING?

It tells it, "You're truly striking!"

WHERE DID MR. COW TAKE MRS. COW FOR A VALENTINE'S DAY DATE?

To the "moo"-vies!

WHY DID THE CHICKEN CROSS THE ROAD?

Because her boyfriend was on the other side.

WHAT IS THE MOST ROMANTIC CITY IN ENGLAND

Loverpool

KNOCK, KNOCK

Who's there?

Woo.

Woo who?

Woo-hoo! Happy Valentine's Day!

WHEN DO VAMPIRES FALL IN LOVE?

At first bite

KNOCK, KNOCK

Who's there?
Candy.
Candy who?
Candy you be my Valentine and make my day sweet?

KNOCK, KNOCK

Who's there?
Butter.
Butter who?
Butter open up, I have a Valentine's Day surprise for you!

KNOCK, KNOCK

Who's there?
Sherwood.
Sherwood who?
Sherwood like to be your Valentine!

HOW CAN YOU TELL THE CALENDAR IS POPULAR?

It has a lot of dates

WHAT DID THE PEAR SAY TO THE OTHER ON VALENTINE'S DAY?

We make the perfect pear

WHAT DID ONE TIGER SAY TO THE OTHER?

I'd be lion if I said I didn't love ya.

HOW DO YOU IMPRESS A BAKER WHEN YOU'RE TAKING HIS DAUGHTER ON A DATE?

Bring her flours.

WHAT DID THE BASEBALL PLAYER SAY TO HIS GIRLFRIEND ON VALENTINE'S DAY?

I pitcher us staying together forever.

KNOCK, KNOCK

Who's there?

Luvs

Luvs who?

Luvs you!

WHAT DID THE ROMANTIC FLEA SAY?

I love you aw-flea!

WHY SHOULD YOU NEVER FALL FOR A TENNIS PLAYER?

Because love means nothing to them!

1 AND 2 FELL IN LOVE.

2 said, you're the only one for me!

WHICH DAY IS THE WORST TO PROPOSE ON?

April Fools' Day!

WHAT DID THE MERMAID SAY TO THE OTHER ON VALENTINE'S DAY?

We are mermaid for each other!

2 BLOOD CELLS MET AND FELL IN LOVE

But, it was all in vein!

WHAT DOES A HEARTBROKEN LEGO PERSON SAY?

I'm falling to pieces!

WHY DID THE ROBOT MARRY HIS PARTNER?

He couldn't resistor!

HOW DO YOU PROPOSE WITH A HELIUM BALLOON?

You pop the question!

ROSES ARE RED,
VIOLETS ARE BLUE.
I'M ALLERGIC TO FLOWERS,
AND MIGHT SNEEZE OVER YOU.

ROSES ARE RED,
VIOLETS ARE BLUE.
I'VE MADE A SANDWICH,
BUT NOT ONE FOR YOU!

ROSES ARE RED,
VIOLETS AREN'T BLUE.
THEY ARE ACTUALLY PURPLE,
THERE'S A FACT FOR YOU!

WHAT DO TWO LEGO PEOPLE IN LOVE SAY?

Never LEGO!

WHAT DID THE GOAT AND ITS DATE WATCH ON VALENTINE'S DAY?

America's Goat Talent!

WHAT DID ONE ELEPHANT SAY TO THE OTHER ON VALENTINE'S DAY?

I love you a ton!

**ROSES ARE RED,
VIOLETS ARE BLUE.
I'M LOOKING FOR A TOILET,
BECAUSE I NEED A POO!**

**ROSES ARE RED,
VIOLETS ARE BLUE
I SAW YOU PICK YOUR NOSE,
EW!**

KNOCK, KNOCK

Who's there?

Frankly.

Frankly, who?

Frankly, I love you.

WHAT DID THE GOAT WITHOUT A VALENTINE'S DAY DATE SAY?

Meehhhhh

WHY DON'T PEOPLE GET MARRIED IN IGLOOS?

In case they get cold feet!

WHAT DID THE EGG SAY TO THE OTHER ON VALENTINE'S DAY?

We make an egg-cellent pair together

WHAT DID THE BEES DO AFTER THEY GOT MARRIED?

They went on a honeymoon.

WHAT DID THE FOOTBALL PLAYER SAY TO HIS GIRLFRIEND ON VALENTINE'S DAY?

I think you might be out of my league.

HOW DID THE COFFEE BEAN EXPRESS ITS LOVE TO THE MUG?

It said, "I love you a latte"

KNOCK, KNOCK

Who's there?

Tank.

Tank who?

Tank you for being my Valentine!

WHAT DID THE ROMANTIC SING AFTER SHE GOT A PAPER CUT?

I keep bleeding, I keep, keep bleeding love

WHAT DID THE HORSE EAT ON FEBRUARY 14?

Valentine's hay

WHAT DID THE DRY GRAPE SAY TO HIS WIFE?

You're the raisin I smile.

WHAT DO YOU CALL THE SMALLEST VALENTINE'S DAY CARD IN THE WORLD?

A Valen-teeny-tiny

WHAT DO YOU GET WHEN YOU CROSS CUPID WITH A BASEBALL PLAYER?

A glover-boy

HOW DOES A VALENTINE ACT WHEN IT'S STUCK IN THE FREEZER?

Cold-hearted

DID YOU HEAR ABOUT THE ROMANCE IN THE TROPICAL FISH TANK?

It was a case of guppy-love

WHAT DID THE BOY SAY TO HIS GIRLFRIEND WHO WORKS AT THE ZOO?

I think you're a keeper

KNOCK, KNOCK

Who's there?

Police

Police who?

Police be my Valentine!

WHAT DID THE BUCK SAY TO THE DOE ON VALENTINE'S DAY?

You're a dear! (Deer)

WHAT DID THE BOY BEAR SAY TO THE GIRL BEAR ON VALENTINE'S DAY?

I wuv you beary much!

WHAT IS A RAM'S FAVORITE SONG?

I only have eyes for ewe, Dear

WHAT DID THE PENCIL SAY TO THE PAPER?

I dot my i's on you!

KNOCK, KNOCK

Who's there?
Jimmy.
Jimmy who?
Jimmy a little kiss?

Who's there?

Atlas.

Atlas who?

Atlas Valentine's Day is here!

WHAT DID THE MOMMY LIZARD WRITE IN A VALENTINE'S CARD FOR HER BABY LIZARD?

You're one in chameleon!

WHAT DID THE WATCH SAY TO HIS GIRLFRIEND?

Will you be my Valen-time?

WHY DID THE MONSTER GET MARRIED?

She met the man of her screams

HOW DID THE SHARK PROPOSE TO HER BOYFRIEND?

I chews you!

KNOCK, KNOCK

Who's there?

Abby

Abby who?

Abby Valentine's Day!

Made in United States
Troutdale, OR
02/05/2024

17469130R00056